9 X 7/09 ✓ 8/09   6/05 (8X) 11/04
21 X 2/10 ✓ 2/11

APATOSAURUS

A TRUE BOOK

by

Elaine Landau

Children's Press®
A Division of Grolier Publishing

New York London Hong Kong Sydney
Danbury, Connecticut

Apatosaurus

Reading Consultant
Linda Cornwell
*Coordinator Of School Quality
And Professional Improvement
Indiana State Teachers Association*

Dedication:
For Cindy Wilson Hyde

Visit Children's Press® on the Internet at:
http://publishing.grolier.com

Library of Congress Cataloging-in-Publication Data

Landau, Elaine.
    Apatosaurus / by Elaine Landau.
      p.   cm. — (A true book)
    Includes bibliographical references (p. -) and index.
    Summary: Describes the physical characteristics, habits, and
natural environment of the huge plant-eating *Apatosaurus* and
discusses theories on why it became extinct.
    ISBN 0-516-20434-3 (lib.bdg.)   0-516-26489-3 (pbk.)
    1. Apatosaurus—Juvenile literature. [1. Apatosaurus.
2. Dinosaurs.] I. Title. II. Series.
QE862.S3L36 1999
567.913'8—dc21   98-24780
                                    CIP
                                    AC

Contents

A Plant-eating Giant

Can you picture the world as it was many millions of years ago? Things looked very different then. The Earth was continually changing.

Separate continents were still forming. There were no humans yet. This was the Mesozoic era, a time also

Apatosaurus was a plant-eating dinosaur.

known as the Age of the
Dinosaurs.

What were dinosaurs?
Dinosaurs were ancient reptiles that lived on land. Like all
reptiles, dinosaurs had scaly
or leathery skin, breathed air
through lungs, and had young

that hatched from eggs with shells.

   This book is about a huge, four-legged, long-necked dinosaur known as *Apatosaurus. Apatosaurus* lived more than 150 million years ago, toward the end of the Jurassic period (the middle portion of the Mesozoic era). *Apatosaurus* was an herbivore— a plant eater. It was among the largest herbivores in the world at that time.

Who Was Apatosaurus?

Apatosaurus looked like what most people think of when they hear the word "dinosaur." It was 70 feet (21 m) long and weighed 30 tons.

This drawing shows how large *Apatosaurus* would have looked next to a 6-foot-tall human.

A full-grown elephant would reach only its hip. One *Apatosaurus* weighed as much as five elephants!

Paleontologists—scientists who study prehistoric life—learn about dinosaurs through fossils. These are dead plant or animal remains that have been preserved in rock over millions of years.

Researchers also find out about dinosaurs through trace fossils. These fossils give clues

Apatosaurus fossil footprints

to how the animal lived. Fossil footprints are trace fossils. A fossil footprint is formed when an animal leaves a footprint in the mud and the mud, over a long time, turns into rock. Fossil footprints can tell us about the animal's size and weight.

Fossils show that *Apatosaurus's* huge body was supported by four massive legs. Its front legs were shorter than its hind ones. This caused the dinosaur's body to slope downward from its hips to its neck.

A fossilized *Apatosaurus* leg bone

Two Names, One Dinosaur

O. C. Marsh (top center) with a student team of fossil hunters

For a long time, *Apatosaurus* was known as *Brontosaurus*. Paleontologist O. C. Marsh described and named *Apatosaurus* in 1877. A few years later, in 1879, he described and named another fossil, *Brontosaurus*. However, it was later discovered that *Brontosaurus* and *Apatosaurus* were actually the same dinosaur. Since the dinosaur had been named *Apatosaurus* first, that's what it is called today.

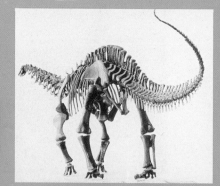

A reconstructed *Apatosaurus* skeleton

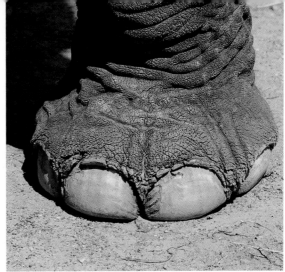

Apatosaurus's feet (left) probably looked similar to those of an elephant (above).

Apatosaurus's short, broad feet have sometimes been compared to an elephant's. Like an elephant, *Apatosaurus* had five stubby toes on each foot. But *Apatosaurus* also had a large claw on the "big toe" of each of its front feet.

Some museum models show this dinosaur with three claws on its hind feet as well. But paleontologists now know that this is incorrect.

Apatosaurus had a long neck and an even longer tail. Its head, however, was extremely small. The average body length of *Apatosaurus* was about 65 feet (20 m). But its head was only 22 inches (55 cm) long! Its entire skull

Apatosaurus had a
small head and a
very long neck.

weighed less than its fourth or
fifth neck bone.

Compared to how the faces
of many animals look today,
Apatosaurus's face might seem
strange. Its eyes were set far

back in its head. Its nostrils were on top of its skull!

Unlike meat-eating dinosaurs, *Apatosaurus* did not have very strong jaws. It had only a few peglike teeth at the front of its jaw. This dinosaur would never be able to rip through a thick animal hide. But its mouth was perfect for pulling leaves off plants.

Apatosaurus's head was small, but its tail was extremely long. It had eighty-two inter-

The long tail of *Apatosaurus* had eighty-two inter-locking bones.

locking bones. The tail narrowed at its end to look like a whip. *Apatosaurus* had a very powerful tail swing. That's because this movement was controlled by the dinosaur's strong back muscles.

Paleontologists believe *Apatosaurus* held its tail off the ground while walking. This might have been a protective measure. If its tail was left to drag along the ground, a shorter animal could bite it, or another *Apatosaurus* might step on it as the herd moved.

How Apatosaurus Lived

Apatosaurus lived in western North America. Its remains have been uncovered in Colorado, Utah, Oklahoma, and Wyoming.

Paleontologists believe *Apatosaurus* did not spend very much time alone.

Area of Detail

UNITED STATES

MONTANA

IDAHO

WYOMING

NEBRASKA

UTAH

COLORADO

KANSAS

ARIZONA

NEW MEXICO

OKLAHOMA

A map showing the states in which fossils of *Apatosaurus* have been found

TEXAS

MEXICO

Apatosaurus may have traveled in herds.

Instead, it probably lived in groups.

Footprints of dinosaurs like *Apatosaurus* show that there might have been as many as twenty *Apatosaurus* in a herd.

Together they roamed the land searching for new feeding grounds.

Being part of a herd was important to *Apatosaurus's* survival. Because it was so big, *Apatosaurus* looked fierce. But if attacked, it was unlikely that this massive creature could outrun its enemy.

Yet this dinosaur was not completely defenseless. It could rear up on its hind legs to thrash an attacker. The claws on its front feet also may have proved useful against an enemy. *Apatosaurus* may even have been able to injure another dinosaur with a swing of its massive tail.

Apatosaurus defending itself against *Allosaurus*

Naturally, there was also safety in numbers. Enemies would be less likely to attack a herd than a lone animal. Paleontologists think that *Apatosaurus* may have acted as elephant herds do when threatened. It probably tried to protect its young. It is possible that the male dinosaurs formed a circle shielding the young dinosaurs and females within.

Apatosaurus may have waded in lakes or rivers.

Apatosaurus was strictly a land animal. It never lived in water. Yet these dinosaurs may have sometimes waded briefly in lakes and rivers. This would have given them a chance to cool off and rinse the dust from their skin.

Feeding Time

Apatosaurus was able to eat a variety of plants. It simply lifted its head to pull leaves from the tallest treetops. Lowering its neck, *Apatosaurus* could graze on low-growing plants and ferns as well.

To support its huge body, *Apatosaurus* probably had to

Apatosaurus probably ate leaves from both tall trees and low-growing plants.

eat throughout the day. There must have been little time for other activities. Unlike flesh-eating dinosaurs, *Apatosaurus* was unable to take huge mouthfuls. Its jaws were too small.

Although *Apatosaurus* had teeth, it did not chew its food. Instead, it swallowed its meals whole. First, however, the dinosaur also swallowed some smooth pebbles. These pebbles are sometimes called

Apatosaurus's teeth were meant for pulling leaves, not for chewing.

"stomach stones." They tore up tough plant matter when it reached the animal's stomach. Once the food was mashed into a thick paste, it was ready to be digested.

Dinosaur National Monument

Apatosaurus actually played a special role in dinosaur history. In 1909, Earl Douglass, a dinosaur researcher from Pittsburgh's Carnegie Museum, was digging for fossils on a sandstone ledge on the Green River in Utah. It was there that he uncovered a nearly complete skeleton of *Apatosaurus*. Thrilled with the finding, Douglass and other Carnegie Museum researchers kept working there. The site proved

This sandstone ledge, now part of Dinosaur National Monument, is rich in dinosaur fossils.

Dinosaur Quarry at Dinosaur National Monument contains many fossils, including those of *Apatosaurus*.

to be rich in fossils, and the dinosaur hunts continued.

But after a while, museum officials grew concerned about others digging at the site. They feared that amateur dinosaur hunters might misuse the fossils. Would these individuals save their findings for scientific research? Or might they simply sell fossils to wealthy private collectors?

The Carnegie Museum was determined to prevent this. They tried to file a claim with the U.S. Department of the Interior to protect the area. But their request was denied.

Fortunately, President Woodrow Wilson came to their aid. On October 4, 1915,

A paleontologist exposing *Apatosaurus* fossils in Dinosaur Quarry

35

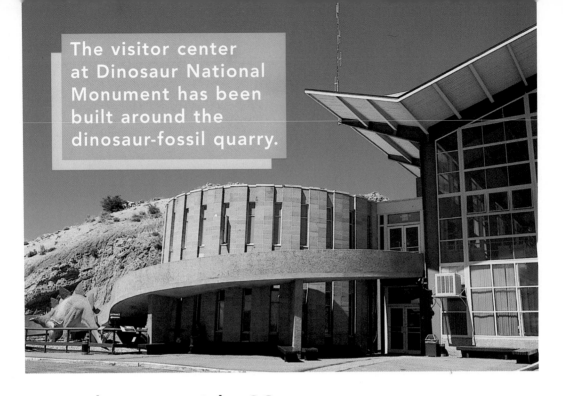

The visitor center at Dinosaur National Monument has been built around the dinosaur-fossil quarry.

he set aside 80 acres (32 hectares) of land in north-western Colorado and north-eastern Utah and named the site Dinosaur National Monument.

Since then, other museums and universities have conducted

dinosaur digs there. Much of the area has been enclosed within a huge permanent building. A dinosaur museum was opened at the site.

Today, visitors to Dinosaur National Monument can see actual fossils. They also can learn about digging up these important clues to the past.

Our Changing World

There are no living dinosaurs left. Today, only skeletons or models of these huge creatures can be seen in museums, theme parks, and movies. Some people mistakenly think that all dinosaurs became extinct at the same

Museum models of *Apatosaurus*

time. But it didn't happen quite that way.

Various types of dinosaurs died out at different stages of the Mesozoic era. None lasted for the whole time that dinosaurs existed on Earth.

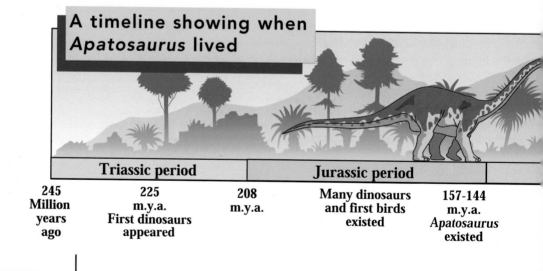

A timeline showing when *Apatosaurus* lived

	Triassic period		Jurassic period	
245 Million years ago	225 m.y.a. First dinosaurs appeared	208 m.y.a.	Many dinosaurs and first birds existed	157-144 m.y.a. *Apatosaurus* existed

In some cases, changes in the climate and environment caused some dinosaurs to become extinct. They were replaced by other animals better able to handle the new conditions.

(Note: "m.y.a." means "million years ago")

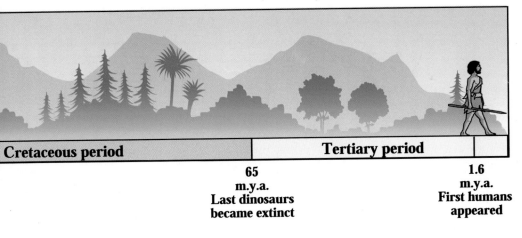

Cretaceous period   Tertiary period

65
m.y.a.
Last dinosaurs
became extinct

1.6
m.y.a.
First humans
appeared

42

Apatosaurus became extinct at the end of the Jurassic period, about 144 million years ago. It is not known why *Apatosaurus* died out when it did. Nevertheless, it lasted on Earth for more than 10 million years. Its fossils have been studied by both past and present-day paleontologists. This giant dinosaur is part of the story of our changing world.

To Find Out More

Here are some additional resources to help you learn more about *Apatosaurus:*

 **Books**

Arnold, Caroline.
  **Dinosaurs All Around:
  An Artist's View of the
  Prehistoric World.**
  Clarion Books, 1993.

Benton, M.J. **How Do We
  Know Dinosaurs
  Existed?** Raintree Steck-
  Vaughn Publications,
  1995.

Brenner, Barbara.
  Dinosaurium. Bantam
  Books, 1993.

Henderson, Douglas.
  Dinosaur Tree. Bradbury
  Press, 1994.

Lindsay, William.
  Prehistoric Life. Knopf,
  1994.

Pringle, Laurence P.
  **Dinosaurs! Strange and
  Wonderful.** Boyd Mills
  Press, 1995.

Simon, Seymour. **New
  Questions and Answers
  about Dinosaurs.**
  Morrow Junior Books,
  1990.

Organizations and Online Sites

The American Museum of Natural History
Central Park West at
79th Street
New York, NY 10024
http://www.amnh.org

One of the world's largest natural-history museums, with exceptional collections on dinosaurs and fossils.

Apatosaurus Page at the Children's Museum of Indianapolis
*http://www.
childrensmuseum.org/
dinoapat.htm*

An *Apatosaurus* information page that includes a picture that you can print out and color yourself.

Dinorama
*http://www.
nationalgeographic.com/
dinorama/frame.html*

A *National Geographic* site with information about dinosaurs and current methods of learning about them. Includes timelines, animations, and fun facts.

Dinosaur National Monument
4545 Highway 40
Dinosaur, CO 81610-9724
http://www.nps.gov/dino/

Visit a unique natural exhibit of more than 1,600 dinosaur bones deposited in an ancient riverbed turned to stone.

National Museum of Natural History, Smithsonian Institution
10th Street and
Constitution Ave. NW
Washington, D.C.
*http://www.mnh.si.edu/
nmnhweb.html*

In the museum's Dinosaur Hall, you can see—and in one case touch—real fossils of dinosaurs.

ZoomDinosaurs
*http://www.
ZoomDinosaurs.com/*

Contains everything you might want to know about dinosaurs and other ancient reptiles. Its *Apatosaurus* page includes facts, myths, activities, a geologic time chart, print-outs, and links.

Important Words

amateur someone who does something without training or skill

continent one of the major land areas of Earth

defenseless not able to defend oneself

extinct something that has died out or no longer exists

interlocking joined or locked together

massive huge

prehistoric existing before humans began recording history

preserve to keep something from being destroyed

reconstructed put back together again

remains bones, tissue, or other matter left behind after an animal or plant dies

shielding protecting or defending something

sprawling spreading or stretched out

Index

Meet the Author

Elaine Landau has a Bachelor of Arts degree in English and Journalism from New York University and a Master's degree in Library and Information Science from Pratt Institute. She has worked as a newspaper reporter, children's book editor, and a youth-services librarian, but especially enjoys writing for young people.

Ms. Landau has written more than a hundred nonfiction books on various topics. She lives in Miami, Florida, with her husband, Norman, and son, Michael.